Vanessa's Book of Awesome Things

RACHEL BARNARD

ISBN: 978-1-944022-00-6

CONTENTS

THE FOOD CHALLENGE

A food challenge, sometimes known as an eating challenge, is a competition to see who can eat or drink a specific (usually large) quantity of a particular food in a particular amount of time.

The original Hero's Bar and Grill food challenge, featured in the book Donuts in an Empty Field (For the Love of Donuts Book 1), is comprised of the following:

- onion rings
- sweet potato fries
- French fries
- burger patties
- mozzarella sticks

Time limit: 20 minutes

TIPS TO HELP YOU WIN A FOOD CHALLENGE

1. Though participating in a food challenge is not necessarily a factor for weight gain, eating a lot and drinking a lot of alcohol may cause you to gain a lot of weight fast.
2. Chew gum to strength train your jaw in preparation.
3. Swallow with your head up during the challenge.
4. Eat the meat(s) and toppings first because they go down faster and easier when fresh.
5. Figure out where your comfort zone is for the challenge: sitting, standing, or kneeling.
6. Use utensils for messy burrito challenges.
7. Dunking is not always necessary (or allowed) but at times it can really help you (especially with burger buns or pizza crust).
8. You can train and build your spice tolerance in preparation (but this can be as slow as training your stomach to expand).
9. After the challenge, eat foods high in dietary fiber to help your digestion.
10. Don't forget to tip your server.

Source:
FoodChallenges.com - Eating Tips, Strategies, & Database. (n.d.). Retrieved September 15, 2015.

10 CHALLENGES AT 10

1	Make paper	
2	Get a manicure	
3	Eat a food you don't like (the entire thing)	
4	Tye dye a shirt	
5	Eat Spam	
6	Dig a 5x5x5 hole	
7	Make a list of 10 things you like about someone and give it to them	
8	Memorize a famous poem or speech from a popular movie	
9	Write your future self a letter	
10	Eat a bug (it can be cooked)	

FACTS ABOUT CORGIS

1. The official dog breed is known as the Welsh Corgi.
2. There are two types: Pembroke and Cardigan.
3. Corgis are known as small Herding Dogs.
4. Average life expectancy is 12-14 years.
5. Corgis are known as active dogs.
6. Corgis are known as vocal dogs.
7. The breed was made popular by Queen Elizabeth II.
8. They shed a lot.
9. Their bellies are low to the ground and get wet.
10. They easily learn new behaviors.

Sources:
So You Think You Want a Corgi. (2011, November 22). Retrieved September 15, 2015.

Welsh Corgi. (n.d.). Retrieved September 15, 2015, from https://en.wikipedia.org/wiki/Welsh_Corgi

20 CHALLENGES AT 20

1	Gallop on a horse	
2	Fast for a day	
3	Donate blood	
4	Swim with dolphins	
5	Ride a Segway	
6	Ride in a limo	
7	Stay awake for 48 hours straight	
8	Participate in a headphone dance party	
9	Spend 3 hours in a Walmart	
10	Go night swimming	
11	Wrestle a friend in the sand	
12	Attempt a world challenge	
13	Make up your own lyrics to a popular song	
14	Participate in a zombie walk	
15	Hide a geocache	

16	Learn a magic trick	
17	Take your parents on a date and pay for everything	
18	Dress up and go out on any day but Halloween	
19	Write a positive note and leave it in a library book	
20	Dumpster dive	

THE SECRET OF TREE BEACH

It's on Longboat Key, right next to the bridge between it and Ana Maria Island. You can get to it by going to St. Armand's Circle and then taking Gulf of Mexico Dr. road that hugs the coast north. That's the scenic view. Or you can take 41 north and turn left (west) on cortez, then turn left again (south) on Gulf of Mexico Dr. You'll pass a super super beach-towny area and then watch for the bridge to Longboat Key. The little beach will be to your right as you cross the bridge going south. Take some seemingly residential road to your right to park - you may have to hunt a little. Also, you'll have to do a bit of walking through mangroves and trees to get to the beach - the anticipation makes it all the better. Tree beach located at the following coordinates:

27°26'23.70"N
82°41'25.05"W

You can park on the side of the dead end road: N. Shore Road off of Gulf of Mexico Dr. on Longboat Key There is a little path on the sand to get to the tree beach area. Don't forget to visit the little tree hut. Parking located at the following coordinates:

27°26'12.28"N
82°41'21.40"W

FAT BOY RUN

A Fat Boy Run, according to Nichole in Donuts in an Empty Field by Rachel Barnard, "It's where you go to a place where there are several fast food restaurants and get one item from each off their value menus."

A Fat Boy Run is a great way to waste time and try something new at the drive thru's of your area.

30 CHALLENGES AT 30

1	Donate $1000	
2	Buy a random stranger a drink	
3	Ride first class in an airplane	
4	Save a life	
5	Play cards or a board game at a local pub	
6	Climb all the stairs in the tallest building in your city	
7	Meet a president	
8	Tour a factory	
9	Do karaoke	
10	Save a tree (or forest)	
11	Learn a bar trick	
12	Take yourself out on a date - by yourself	
13	Design your dream house	

14	Harvest your own garden	
15	Write a nice letter to a random address in your town and mail it to them	
16	Make a nice meal and give it to a homeless person	
17	Read the entire Bible or other religious text	
18	Pie/cake someone in the face	
19	Do a 2000 piece puzzle	
20	Sleep outside without a tent	
21	Punch someone in the face/get punched in the face	
22	Try the hottest sauce your town has to offer	
23	Make grass angels	
24	Buy out a lemonade stand (or girl scout stand/hot dog stand/etc)	

25	Buy an original painting	
26	Go on the one ride at an amusement park that scares you	
27	Be a character in a haunted house	
28	Patent/trademark something	
29	Make soap	
30	Write a book or short story	

YOUR LOCAL HANGOUT

Nichole and Vanessa have a local hangout at the church within walking distance to both their houses in Donuts in an Empty Field.

Your local hangout should be accessible and easy to get to, ideally within walking distance. It should have a place to park and a place to sit and chat. Ideally it would be publically accessible.

The church hangout in the book is full of neat things. It doubles as a school and features a nativity set during the holiday season. There is a small playground out back and access to some maze-like woodsy areas behind the buildings.

40 CHALLENGES AT 40

1	Watch a roller derby bout	
2	Participate in a food fight	
3	Participate in a color run	
4	Tear a phone book in half	
5	Shoot a gun	
6	Go to a wine tasting	
7	Eat cake with your hands	
8	Make ice cream	
9	Go out with a friend and wear the exact same outfit	
10	Spend a day talking in a different accent	
11	Spend a day without saying a word	
12	Learn a popular dance (thriller/harlem shake/etc)	
13	Plank or owl in public	

14	Go spelunking	
15	Go primitive Camping	
16	Swing from a rope into a lake or river	
17	Go on a road trip	
18	Master a yoga pose	
19	Visit a medieval/renaissance village	
20	Watch a joust	
21	Release a balloon into the ' air in remembrance of someone important in your life	
22	Donate hair	
23	Learn how to crack an egg with one hand	
24	Mimic Chopped or other fun food show challenge	
25	Visit a famous movie filming location	
26	Make apple cider	

27	Create your own unique recipe	
28	Ride a penny-farthing	
29	Ride a unicycle	
30	Ride a tandem bike	
31	Have breakfast in bed	
32	Ride a train	
33	Go on a helicopter tour	
34	Swim in a fountain	
35	Participate in a flash mob	
36	Do the top 5 tourist things in your city or state	
37	Go out in your pajamas	
38	Get a caricature	
39	Participate in No Shave November	
40	Make up your own mixed drink/cocktail	

REASONS TO BASK IN A SEA OF PUPPIES

1. It can be therapeutic.
2. Who wouldn't want to get accidentally peed on by more than one puppy at the same time?
3. You can boast about it.
4. It is the cutest thing you will ever do.
5. Puppies are soft.
6. The puppies will lick and love on you.
7. Puppies need socializing too.

50 AT 50

1	Create a bucket list	
2	Visit a castle	
3	Ride in a hot air balloon	
4	Give a $100 tip	
5	Give someone you love a dozen roses for no reason other than you love them	
6	Write a letter to the editor	
7	Host a themed party	
8	Go to a cake tasting	
9	Make an unboxing video	
10	Win a scratch lottery	
11	Hold a tarantula	
12	Buy a stranger a cup of coffee	
13	Try an art class	
14	Take a bartending class	

15	Participate in April Fool's	
16	Attend a murder mystery dinner	
17	Write one of your old high school friends a letter	
18	Participate in talk like a pirate day	
19	Pay for a stranger's groceries	
20	Draw/paint a self-portrait	
21	Watch every James Bond movie	
22	Drive on a race track	
23	Be in a TV audience	
24	Walk across a famous bridge	
25	Stay overnight in a haunted hotel	
26	Watch the sun rise and set on the same day	
27	Go to a toastmasters meeting	
28	Get a crazy haircut	

29	Visit a nudist beach	
30	Get a giant turkey leg at a renaissance fair	
31	Go to a drive in movie	
32	Go to the local farmer's market	
33	Make your own soup	
34	Volunteer to be a docent at the local museum	
35	Try laughter yoga	
36	Write your autobiography	
37	Go on an A to Z food tour	
38	Take a walking tour of your town	
39	Take a cooking class	
40	Participate in an open mic	
41	Rent a jet ski	
42	Attend a local food/wine tasting festival	

43	Rent the car you always wanted to buy and never did	
44	Sit in a hot tub in the rain	
45	Participate in a pub crawl	
46	Get your fortune told	
47	Attend a movie premier	
48	Be a vegan for a week	
49	Go to a cat café	
50	Make homemade dog treats	

KALE IS NOT A CURSE WORD

1. What the kale?
2. Kale that!
3. Kale yeah!
4. Go to kale!
5. A kale of a mess.
6. Shot to kale.
7. Give someone kale.
8. All kale breaks loose.
9. Kale hath no fury…
10. Kale of a time.
11. Don't have a hope on kale.
12. Sure as kale.
13. The road to vegans is paved with good kale.
14. You scared the kale out of me!
15. Don't give a kale.
16. When kale hits the dinner table.
17. When kale takes over.
18. Kale you!
19. Go kale yourself!
20. Kale a whale!
21. If that don't kale all!
22. Kale it, kale happens, move along.

DOUGHNUTS RECIPE

Doughnut Recipe by Khiel Barnard

Ingredients:
- 1 1/2 cups flour
- 2 tablespoons sugar
- pinch of salt
- 1/2 cup warm water
- 1/2 tablespoon yeast
- 1 egg
- honey, maple, syrup, powdered sugar, or chocolate chips for toppings
- vegetable oil, olive oil or Avocado Oil

1. Add yeast to warm water and mix
2. Combine dry ingredients: flour, salt and sugar
3. Slowly combine egg, then yeast-water mixture until dough starts to form
4. Kneed for 10 minutes (add flour or water as needed to keep dough a light and fluffy consistency)
5. Cover with tin foil so that no air may get in or out (anaerobic environment)
6. Place on top of fridge for 1 hour
7. Fill small stainless steel pot with 2 inches of oil and heat on medium low heat until bubbles form on surface
8. Cut dough into 5" X 1"strips then form around finger into ringlets
9. Place 1 or 2 at a time in oil for 25-30 seconds on each side
10. Cover with toppings or melted chocolate chips (easy to melt in butter in a bowl in the microwave)
11. Eat warm or let cool.

OBJECT SCAVENGER HUNT

Must bring back 15/20 of the following items

1	Rock shaped like a heart	
2	Egg shaped rock	
3	Shell	
4	Sand	
5	Purple flower	
6	Ticket stub	
7	Candy wrapper	
8	Tennis ball or other used dog toy	
9	Yellow leaf	
10	Very dirty penny	
11	Stamp	
12	Check deposit slip	
13	Chinese takeout menu	
14	Shoelace	
15	Paperclip	

16	Golf tee	
17	Lego	
18	Hair tie	
19	Cigarette butt	
20	Rock shaped like a heart	

PHOTO SCAVENGER HUNT

Must take photographs of 20/25 of the following:

1	A pregnant lady	
2	A baby	
3	A dog	
4	A terribly dressed person	
5	An impeccably dressed person	
6	A couple making out	
7	Someone giving you a sign (peace/the finger)	
8	A classic novel	
9	A mannequin	
10	On a swing set	
11	Someone in a uniform	
12	A city bus	
13	A sports jersey or hat	

14	Someone in scrubs	
15	A street musician	
16	Phone booth	
17	Water fountain	
18	A guy in a dress	
19	A muscle car	
20	An elevator/escalator	
21	Someone doing a handstand	
22	Your doppelganger	
23	Pinball machine or other arcade game	
24	Photo booth	
25	A convertible.	

TO DO WITH DONUTS, YES OR NO?

1	Eat them	
2	Stack them	
3	Flatten them	
4	Play ring toss with them	
5	Propose with them	
6	Use them as telescopes	
7	Use them as hats	
8	Use them as gambling currency	
9	Make them into bread pudding	
10	Microwave them	

TOP TEN WORST DONUT FLAVORS

1	Mimosa Flavored Donut	
2	Deep Fried Kool-Aid Balls	
3	Donut with Bugs on Top	
4	Maple Spam Donut	
5	Gooey Butter Donut	
6	Bar Snack Donut	
7	Sour Cream and Onion Donut	
8	Pulled Pork and Potato Salad Donut	
9	Jager Bomb Donut	
10	Rock Candy Donut	

TOP TEN DONUTS YOU HAVE TO TRY

1	Taro-Flavored Donut	
2	French Toast Donut	
3	Maple Bacon Donut	
4	Grilled Cheese Donut	
5	Green Tea Donut	
6	Nerds Topped Donut	
7	Peanut Butter and Jelly Donut	
8	Peeps Donut	
9	Krispy Kreme Burger	
10	Croissant Donut	

BONUS BUCKET LIST ITEMS

1	Go on a blind date	
2	Been handcuffed to a partner/friend for 24 hours	
3	Gone on a cruise	
4	Scuba diving	
5	Win a food challenge	
6	Participated in a sober morning dance rave	
7	Fired a gun	
8	Paid only using coins	
9	Served on a jury	
10	Ridden a motorcycle	

ABOUT DONUTS BY GUEST AUTHOR RACHEL RADTKE

One of the most enticing things about donuts, is the way they get away with things. Donuts start out as naughty sugar morsels. Then, they get dipped in glaze, slathered with chocolate, topped with sprinkles, or filled with custard. But that only refers to the most humdrum of donuts. Look further and you'll find delicacies topped with bacon, filled with a range of velvety mousse flavors, even indulgences that are so over the top they must be eaten with a fork. And yet, donuts are considered a breakfast food. In a world of "breakfast is the most important meal of the day", donuts managed to weasel its way onto the table alongside respectable breakfast cuisine such as eggs, yogurt, and fruit. Now, it's not like all traditional breakfast foods are pillars of nutrition. Nobody really thinks a bowl of marshmallow cereal really is the healthiest start to the day. Yet we have marketing campaigns dedicated to "whole grain" this and "fiber" that, desperate to assuage our guilt, and convince us that milk poured over sugar confers magical health-giving powers. But not donuts. Donuts don't lie. Donuts don't manipulate. Donuts are arguably, and unapologetically, solidly in the "dessert" category, yet get away with being an acceptable breakfast food in a way no other confection could pull off. Ice cream? Never. Cake? Maybe, but only the day after your birthday. Cookies? Brownies? Better wait until lunch. But when it comes to donuts, the rules change. Hey, jelly filled counts as a serving of fruit, right?

SEATTLE CHECKLIST

1	Bunny Yoga	
2	Cat Café	
3	Gum Wall	
4	Kombucha Bar	
5	Stand Up Paddleboard Yoga	
6	Cupcake Phone	
7	Molly Moon's Ice Cream	
8	Fremont Troll	
9	Seattle Metaphysical Library	
10	Bicycle Tree on Vashon Island	

FOR THE LOVE OF DONUTS BOOKS

Donuts in an Empty Field
(For the Love of Donuts Book One)

Letting go of anger is life's greatest challenge.

Vanessa Smith hasn't been the same since her father's death. A hero until the end, he died saving a restaurant owner's wife and son from a burning building. Nessa has always blamed the boy, Ben, for her loss, and her thoughts are consumed with ways to make him as miserable as she is.

Best friend Nichole Adams knows Nessa can never heal until she learns to let go of her hatred, but bringing back her best friend is proving more difficult than she could've imagined. In a last ditch effort to break Nessa's obsession, Nichole hopes signing up for the local food challenge is just the thing to bust her out of her shell.

A single choice defines the road ahead for Nessa. Doing the right thing isn't easy, but living with the consequences of doing nothing might be worse.

DONUTS IN AN EMPTY FIELD
CHAPTER ONE - MEMENTOS

We haven't opened this room in five years.

"Are you sure you're up for this, Vanessa?" Mom asks.

I nod, but I'm not ready. How can I deal? Dad could be alive if he hadn't tried to be a hero.

I glance back at Mom and take a deep breath before I grab the office doorknob, turn, and push.

The smell hits me. Stale. Musty. Humid.

This is not how I remember Dad.

I hold my breath and look around, trying to recall the distinct way he smelled. This used to be Dad's office. Now it's a stagnant room full of useless things. Things we're going to get rid of. All his books and papers and desk toppers. Junk crammed onto a six-foot desk and packed into a room that is little bigger than a walk in closet.

Mom pats me on the back and I step inside. Letting out a breath with a whoosh, I tiptoe around piles of books on the floor and sit in the office chair. It creaks backwards. Mom stands in the middle of the room with her hands clasped tight together in front of her stomach. Thin streams of sunlight filter through the blinds, highlighting the dust motes in the air.

Bluster noses his way into the room, waddling around to sniff at each pile of books and papers stacked on the floor. I bend down to pet him. Not only is it the anniversary of my father's death, but it's

also the anniversary of the day we got Bluster. It's almost as if he came to replace Dad, arriving mere hours ahead of the incident at the restaurant. Bluster's stubby reddish brown tail beats at my thigh as I try to hold him down and hug him. Bluster's softness rubs against my bare legs. I can hear his heartbeat pattering and his breath wheezing as he struggles to get out of my grip. He smells like a dog should, musty wet from his recent bath. I breathe deep, the smell overpowering the staleness of the office around us.

When Dad brought home Bluster five years ago, I was thrilled. Corgi pups are divine and I was absolutely smitten with the little guy. I'm certain it was the reason boys never interested me until later. From the first tail-wag, mess on the floor, and sharp bark, I was in love.

Mom only shook her head and sighed. Dad was forever surprising both of us with shenanigans. He usually got away with them, too. I dropped hints for years about wanting a dog, but Mom always said no. It was much harder to say "no" to the dog's face.

Bluster and I bonded the minute Dad set him into my arms. No matter how much Mom didn't want a dog, she couldn't take him away from me because Bluster was the last present Dad ever gave me.

Shoes tap in the main part of the house on our wood floors and my best friend Nichole appears in the doorway. She glances at Mom and then locks eyes with me, looking down at me from her model height of 5'8". She hesitates outside the door, still holding my gaze with her own brown eyes. She twirls a slender finger through her shoulder length brown hair with blonde highlights and chews on her lip.

"Are you sure that it's okay for me to be here?" Nichole asks.

I nod and she steps inside, her heels tapping on the wood floor without rhythm as she takes tentative steps.

"Thank you for coming. Of course it's okay. Vanessa and I very much appreciate you helping out," Mom says.

I frown. "We don't have to do this."

Nichole says at the same time, "It's okay, I wanted to help."

We look at each other. Normally we're more in sync, but today everyone's rhythm is off.

"Thanks, Nichole," I sigh.

She remains silent, waiting for Mom to be the parent and say something helpful.

Mom shakes her head. "It's time." She sighs heavily and unclasps her hands. Mom wears no makeup and her eyelids droop. Her lips are a thin, pale line without lipstick. I have Mom's hair, at least when she was younger, but I don't have to dye mine to keep its dark brunette color.

Nichole purses her lips and I internally roll my eyes at Mom's lack of parental guidance. At the very least, she usually gives me the canned therapy version of sympathy and support, but today is hard for her too.

Mom sweeps her hair over her shoulders, out of her pale face, revealing the too-large ears I inherited. She steps back into the hall to pick up the cleaning supplies we'd forgotten outside the room. Bluster looks up at me and whines. I pet him and he settles down onto the

floor.

Touching Dad's precious books and trinkets makes his presence feel closer than it has felt in years, like he could walk in and tell us the corgi bobblehead doesn't belong in a box, but front and center on his desk next to his donut patterned mouse pad. Putting his stuff in a box is like putting him and my memories of him into a box. I don't want to forget Dad, but both Mom and my therapist agreed it's time to donate the books and clean out the office. That it has to be done. In a single story house with three bedrooms and an office, we sure don't need the space. I don't understand why today, of all days it has to be done, but it isn't my choice. Mom wants to get it over with. She has plans tomorrow. I don't have enough energy to object.

"So," Nichole says into the silence. "I'm glad you have the air-conditioning on, it's hot out there." She wipes the back of her hand over her forehead. Her cheeks are sun-tanned, slightly darker than her normal olive skin tone. We're both of mixed European heritage, but Nichole got genes for tanning and I didn't.

"It's Florida in the summer. Of course it's hot," I say. I get up out of the office chair, releasing a puff of dust.

Mom starts with the pictures. Photos clutter Dad's desk and windowsill, overlapping with smiles and memories. My heart constricts tighter and tighter with every photo placed face down in one of the medium-sized boxes Mom dragged in. I don't want to cry in front of Nichole. If I'm too much of a bother, she might leave and hang out with her other friends, doing

something more fun.

The sun creates shadows through the dusty blinds, striping on the box like a jail cell. I apologize silently to Dad's memory as I nestle in each new photo.

"Do you want to keep any, Vanessa?" Mom asks.

I look at the collection of bobble heads on his desk, the Rubik's cubes and desktop puzzles, the office toys. They don't remind me of Dad the way Bluster does. They don't mean more than my memories of him. I shake my head at Mom and she tilts her head, regarding me, before settling back into the routine of placing odds and ends from the desk into boxes.

Then I see the last photograph.

It's a larger picture, printed at home and tacked onto the corkboard in a hurry. On Dad's last day alive, after he'd surprised me with the dog, he took us to Sarasota's only dog park. Bluster was six months old, still small enough for me to hold him tight to my chest without his legs falling out of my arms, but old enough to mingle with the park's smaller dogs. We'd gone to the dog park to let Bluster socialize and Dad was going to break the world record for most powdered donuts eaten in three minutes. After Bluster wore himself out, we put him back on the leash and left the dog area to find ourselves a secluded picnic table.

The picture was taken after Dad failed. Powdered sugar coated Dad's beard, the top of Bluster's head, even dusting the park bench and floating to the ground below. Mom kept trying to wipe powdered sugar off Dad's beard.

Dad had no qualms asking a stranger to take our

photo. It was frustrating that I couldn't even remember if the stranger had been a man or a woman.

I remember Dad.

Dad was an inch or two above average height, about 6 feet tall, and had the regular dad paunch that signifies the presence of children who never finish their own dinner and give leftovers to Dad to eat. He was always trying to talk or wave to strangers. Everyone always recognized Dad for his friendliness. I wonder if it was to show me that good people exist in the world. That I could be one of them.

I reach up to pull the photo off the corkboard, but my hand stops halfway. I can't do it. This is still Dad's office, in some way, and the picture belongs here.

Mom smiles at the picture, but her eyes still droop and her lips are so thin they almost disappear into her mouth.

"It'll get better," Mom says.

"You still have each other," Nichole offers. "And you have me," she adds.

"I know."

"This is really hard for both of us." Mom looks away. "I've scheduled you with Dr. Bryan later today while I'm out with Walter."

"Your new boyfriend, right?" Nichole asks.

Mom won't meet my gaze. I know this is hard for her, too. I try to give her a break for setting up a dating profile online. For abandoning me on the hardest weekend of the year for a date. I'm mad at her for being so open about dating again, for telling me about it and expecting me to accept that she's moved on

when I haven't.

"Walter has been helping me get through this, too."

Nichole looks at me for an explanation, but I don't want to get into the argument about Mom dating again right now.

"I'm kind of hungry, Mrs. S.," Nichole says, sensing our discomfort.

Mom nods absently.

"How 'bout a snack Mrs. Smith," Nichole says louder.

Mom shakes her head as if to clear away her thoughts. "Sure, be right back girls."

Nichole waits until Mom's out of the room to start shoving books into another larger box.

"Hey," I say.

Nichole pauses and stands up straight to regard me. "What? You're dragging this out and it's not going to get easier the longer you do it. Let's get it over with."

Nichole walks over to me, reaches up to grab the photograph off the wall and I slap her arm away.

"Seriously? Come on Vanessa."

"Don't you dare. You can't just walk in here and throw his stuff into boxes like it's junk."

Nichole raises her eyebrows and takes a step back.

"That's not what I-"

"I'm going to leave this one," I say with a scowl.

Nichole holds up her hands in surrender.

"Fine," she says.

I reach up to touch the photograph, fingering one of the loose corners at the bottom. Peripherally I see

Nichole take another step back, watching the wall and my finger.

She trips over a stack of books on the floor. I don't think. Swiveling to help her, my finger is still hooked around the edge of the picture. It rips as I leap sideways to grab at Nichole's flailing arms. She backpedals over the stack of books. I yank her back to the open floor and let go of her arm. The ripped corner of the photo clutched in my fingers flutters to the ground.

Nichole sucks in a breath as I turn to face the ruined picture. Something flutters behind the missing corner and I lift the stiff paper to peer behind it.

Something is there.

Nichole and I both jump at the sound of a crash from the front of the house.

"Mom!" I yell.

I'm wound up from being in Dad's office, from remembering our last day together, to the finality of packing up his stuff that I go into panic mode and run toward the door. Nichole bumps into me in our haste to make sure Mom's okay and we both fall to the floor. My world turns upside down and I bang my head against Nichole's knee. I'm panting and scrambling to disentangle my limbs from Nichole's. Mom still hasn't answered.

We run out to see what happened. Mom's in the kitchen, her hands braced on opposite sides of the sink. For a moment I'm immensely angry that she didn't answer when I called, scaring the bejesus out of Nichole and me, but then I notice she's crying. Shame

at my anger crashes down on my shoulders.

"Give us a minute?" I ask Nichole.

She nods and heads back to the office. I wince at the sounds of books smacking into one other as Nichole throws them into boxes.

"Mom?"

"It just slipped," she says without looking up.

Several large pieces of one of our flowered yellow and green plates are on the ground next to Mom. We've never broken any of the plates before.

Thankfully, I'm wearing my favorite pair of Crocs, and I don't have to leave Mom alone right now to go get shoes. I can see smaller pieces of the ceramic littering the floor in between tufts of Bluster's fur and crumbs from our last meal.

"It's okay, Mom."

I bend in to hug her and she turns to me with shaking shoulders, sniffling and blinking to stop her tears.

"It'll get easier," I tell her, patting her on the back.

"Grief is a funny thing. It's never the same and it's always a tough upward climb, but you'll get there. It won't be easy, but you're strong and you'll get through it," Mom assures me, turning back into the parent.

Ugh. There's the canned therapy talk. At least she's feeling more like herself, even if I don't.

I notice she doesn't include herself in the statement.

"Don't you miss him?"

"Of course I miss him; he was your father." She sighs out.

The anger knots tight, pressed up against the agony and emptiness Dad left behind. He wasn't just my father; he was Mom's husband. He had friends. He was a part of my world and now he's pictures and mementos and everything I still remember about him, and more that I can't.

I don't want to replace Dad, but I want to move on. I put on a brave face, masking my emotions as best I can and say, "Nichole and I can take care of the rest of Dad's stuff."

"Thank you, Vanessa," Mom agrees.

Dad wouldn't have wanted me to get upset at Mom, especially since she's also sad today. I grab her shoes for her. She smiles at me with another sigh.

"You go ahead with Nichole. I'm going to clean this up first. Here." Mom hands me a bag of carrots and some homemade hummus. "For Nichole and for you if you get hungry." She glances at my stomach tight against my shirt and I suck in reflexively. Even on this bad day, she has to remind me that I'm overweight.

I take the snack and walk back to the office. Nichole sits in the chair, using her feet to swivel herself back and forth as she holds something in her hands.

"What, break time already?" I ask. The anger knots tighter.

Nichole drops the piece of paper onto the desk and I can't help but watch is it flutters back and forth before settling off-kilter near the edge.

"What does it say?" I ask.

"I don't know." Nichole hands it to me. It's a lined notebook paper with a bunch of scribbles. Sorrow hits me. I don't recognize the handwriting, but it has his name at the top, under the date.

The numbers blur as I hold back the tears. I've forgotten another part of my memories of Dad.

I read through the scribbles and turn to Nichole in confusion. I show her the note.

July 22, 2002
1. ~~Get a dog~~
2. Win a food challenge.
3. Shoot a gun.
4. Ride a motorcycle.
5. Skydive.
6. Perform a kind deed without expecting anything in return.

"It's a bucket list," she explains.

"But why?"

"What do you mean, why? Most people have them," Nichole says.

"Not my dad. He would have told me."

Nichole gives me a funny look. "Seems like your dad though. I mean, c'mon, win a food challenge?"

"Yeah, it does kind of sound like him. But only one has been crossed out." I frown, thinking of everything Dad never got a chance to accomplish. Did he even get a chance to try half of these things? "The day he died." I gulp and close my eyes for a long blink. "The

day he died, he was trying to beat the world record for most donuts eaten in three minutes. I remember that day. Almost every detail. Why isn't that on this list, why the generic food challenge?"

Nichole doesn't answer and I continue. "He took us, Mom, Bluster and I to the dog park. He was always into getting things done. A dog and donuts on the same day, in the same place. I remember he let me hold the timer. It made me feel important."

Nichole nods.

"He wasn't very good at eating donuts fast, but he made us laugh. He was covered in powdered sugar and it made me think of Christmas snow. I was proud and embarrassed for Dad at the same time. He was so fun, but he was always doing weird things."

Nichole inclines her head at my words and gets out of the office chair. She paces the room twice and then starts methodically and carefully putting books into boxes.

"I remember I could taste the powdered sugar. He was eating so fast that it was poofing everywhere. Bluster kept winding his leash under his legs as he watched us. Mom and I both laughed at Dad. He managed to swallow the first donut and was already stuffing the second one into his mouth."

I stop my story and sigh. Nichole looks up at me.

"I'm listening," she says.

"There was no way he was going to beat the record and I teased him the rest of the day for failing. Now, I wish I hadn't." I look down at my hands, Dad's bucket list clenched in them.

"You should do it," Nichole declares.

"What?"

"You should do his bucket list."

"What? No way."

Mom appears in the doorway. I slide the paper under a stack of folders on the desk.

"Everything alright?" she asks.

Nichole looks at me and I shrug.

"Here, I'll take the boxes out to the car," she offers.

She lifts one of the heavier, book-filled boxes and staggers out. I'm glad we're donating his books, but I'm sad to see them go. The room is empty without them.

"Are you going to tell her about the list?" Nichole asks.

I consider it. "No. I don't think so." I don't want to share this piece of Dad with anyone else. Mom would make me share it with my therapist. She would minimize it and then disappear on a date.

"Well, I'm pooped. Do you want me to stick around?" Nichole asks.

"Ugh no, Mom scheduled a session for me later this afternoon. Why can't she just pull me out of class like all the other parents so I can at least skip school?" The humor sounds foreign to my ears because I'm still reeling from cleaning out Dad's office and having to comfort Mom.

I retrieve the list from under the files and walk up to take down the photograph from the corkboard. I want to move on. Nichole ushers me out of the room,

clutching the unopened bag of carrots, Bluster following behind us. I clutch both the bucket list and the ripped photograph in my hands as she shuts the door firmly behind us.

Purchase Donuts in an Empty Field (For the Love of Donuts Book 1) from Amazon

http://amzn.to/2dsXjEg

OTHER BOOKS BY RACHEL BARNARD

At One's Beast
Young Adult
Fairy Tale Adaptation
Low Fantasy
Love Triangle
Available in print, e-book, and as an audiobook

Wandering Imagination
A small book of poems that almost got away.

Ataxia and the Ravine of Lost Dreams
Young Adult
Dystopian
Action & Adventure
A hint of Romance
A bit of Science Fiction.
Available in print, e-book, and as an audiobook.

<u>At One's Beast by Rachel Barnard</u>

From once upon a time to happily ever after, At One's Beast highlights the struggles of two young adolescents who have fallen prey to chance evil circumstances. When it took the entire village to create the monster, what will it take to break the spell?

Available in print, e-book, and as an audio book, At One's Beast is a new take on "Beauty and the Beast," with a love triangle, revenge, a spell, evil, fate, forgiveness, compassion, bitterness, capture, betrayal and love.

<u>Ataxia and the Ravine of Lost Dreams by Rachel Barnard</u>

In Ataxia and the Ravine of Lost Dreams A young girl takes on the mighty powers of the government but is sidetracked by challenges of the academy she attends, the new boy, and keeping her secrets safe.

She will do anything - forfeit her identity, friendships, even love - to be humanity's champion.

As the U.S. government prepares to take over the world, MC infiltrates one of their elite academies that trains future leaders. MC must rise to the top in the Cube training grounds in order to be placed high up within the government so she can stop it in its takeover.

It is not until her fourth and final year at the academy that her top-student status is threatened by the sudden arrival of Li, the new transfer student. MC is completely focused on her self-created mission until she gets sidetracked by Li, who might be bad news in more ways than which she bargained.

A Young Adult, Dystopian, Not-So-Distant-Future Adventure Novel with a hint of sci-fi and a bit of romance.

ABOUT THE AUTHOR

I am an author
I am a geocacher
I am an ice cream lover
I am efficient
I am an idea generator
I am impatient
I am loyal
I am hazel eyed
I am a wearer of fuzzy socks
I am a Pinewood Derby and Boot Tossing Winner
I am someone with stage fright
I am learning
I am color coding my calendar
I am clever
I am a blogger
I am a reader
I am an Indie supporter
I am a dancer
I am compiling and listing and analyzing
I am not a fish

Favorite word: sesquipedalian
Favorite type of donut: old-fashioned
Favorite movie: Wedding Singer
Favorite scent: sleep
Favorite item to collect: chapstick
Favorite fruit: peach

Dear Future Self,

It is the year 2025. One year before it all goes down in that first book you wrote, Ataxia was it? So hard to keep track after the first twenty books. Whew! After you became a national bestseller you quit all your day jobs and started cranking out multiple books every year, becoming a writer hermit. Go out! You're too pale. Get some sun.

You're such a sellout. You did a deal with Dunkin Donuts and your For the Love of Donuts Series is all about the donuts now. All your book signings happen in their stores, it's really weird and you have to sign all these sticky books, but hey free donuts for life ain't bad, right?

You need to stop wearing that ghillie suit to all your other appearances, it's really freaking out your mother. And people keep stepping on you. That's how you broke your toe the first time.

Don't forget the little people, ok? Fame and fortune will try to get to your head, but I know you can stay within reality. A reality that includes donuts for life, a marshmallow room, and a staircase made out of books. You're welcome.

Sincerely,
    Rachel Barnard   7/24/15
    From the Future

www.ingramcontent.com/pod-product-compliance
Lightning Source LLC
Chambersburg PA
CBHW051047030426
42339CB00006B/234